The
LIGHT
—in—
DARKNESS

IKE WILLIAMS

Copyright © 2024 Ike Williams.

All rights reserved. No part of this book may be reproduced, stored, or transmitted by any means—whether auditory, graphic, mechanical, or electronic—without written permission of both publisher and author, except in the case of brief excerpts used in critical articles and reviews. Unauthorized reproduction of any part of this work is illegal and is punishable by law.

ISBN: 979-8-89031-991-3 (sc)
ISBN: 979-8-89031-992-0 (hc)
ISBN: 979-8-89031-993-7 (e)

Because of the dynamic nature of the Internet, any web addresses or links contained in this book may have changed since publication and may no longer be valid. The views expressed in this work are solely those of the author and do not necessarily reflect the views of the publisher, and the publisher hereby disclaims any responsibility for them.

One Galleria Blvd., Suite 1900, Metairie, LA 70001
(504) 702-6708

Contents

Foreword ix
Acknowledgments xi

1
GONE BUT NOT FORGOTTEN

Ode To My Mother 3
Ode To My Brother 5

2
RHYTHMS OF LIFE

Life 9
In This Town 10
Rhythm of Life 11
Gone Too Soon 12
Born To Die 13

3
UNLOVED

The Meeting 17
I Name Man! 18
The Mirror and I 19
Missing 22

4
SUFFERING

The Pain of Emptiness 25
Cry of the Masses 28
Trapped 30
I Cry To Myself 31
Reading Rapp 32
The Old Blind Beggar 34
Sing! Sing! Africa! 36
Flesh And Spirit 38

5
ESCAPE

Frozen People, Frozen Town 41
A Stranger In The Land 42
Chasing After You! 43
Free 45

*This work is dedicated to all the members of Self Theatrical Movement
which was founded in Spanish Town Jamaica in 1973
Though Self no longer exists in that location as an institution, the
spirit of the movement is scattered to different parts of the world by
those who came under the influence and whose destinies were changed
as our lives collided and caused us to re-invent ourselves.
The experience with the various personalities in the group extracted
from my deepest soul, creativity, determination, courage and
endurance and provided for me the environment for self expression
which has helped to shape me into the person that I am today.
I thank them for allowing me to use their lives and
artistic energies to grow the seed in me.*

*Many life lessons were learned in our rap sessions
and problem solving discussions.
There are former members today like myself whose heart still
burn with the passion of something unexplainable. The desire
to transcend and leave our plot lovelier then we found it.
My brothers and sisters wherever you are today,
let us continue this journey in love.
God is love.*

Foreword

The poems in this collection were written over many years at different times in the writer's life experiences. Most however were written in the Bahamas between 1987 – 2013 for church groups, schools and theatre groups.

But 'Rhythm of life', 'Cry of the Masses', 'This Town', and 'Frozen People', were written in Jamaica for Self Theatrical Movement.

A Stranger in the Land, The Blind Beggar, Reading Rapp and Chasing After You, were written on my return home, in 2014.

The **'Light In darkness'** collection is a reminder that in our lives there will be moments of darkness and desperation. But hope will always emerge out of every dark situation like a light, so long as we don't give up or think that all is lost.

In God there is no darkness, and "all things work together for good……" *Romans 8:V 28*

"There is no pit so deep, that God's love is not deeper still" – *Corrie ten Boom*

Acknowledgments

I would like to thank all the members of Self Theatrical Company, the many schools and community groups that I have worked with over the years in different places, writing scripts and directing plays, which opened the pathway for me to put together some of my works in this collection of poems.

1

GONE BUT NOT FORGOTTEN

Ode To My Mother

From humble beginnings she came
Inez was her name
My mother so special to me
An only child, who knew no father
Her mother's only daughter.

Her hair was styled the same odd way
From day to day
When she went to work wearing blue attire
The uniform of the working class

From work to church the life she led
So simple and contented
She had not much
But made no fuss
Making difficult ends to meet.

I often gaze on her lovely face
As I listen to her sweet and gently voice
Singing as she cooked and cleaned
And often wondered what a star she'd be

If were not held back by poverty.
Oh mother, dear sweet mother
So many words come to mind
To describe your personality

Independent, kind and forgiven
You stood up when you were falling down
Loyal, honest and consistent
You made lemonade when handed lemons.
Oh mother, dear sweet mother
You are gone but never will be forgotten.

Ode To My Brother

Brother man, Rasta man
That's who he grew up to be
Mother teaching us to be a brother's keeper
And to cover each other's nakedness.

Mother loved him very much
She coined a special name for him
'ohlo'
Which made him smile when he was called.

He was the mirror image of our father
Whom mother loved like no other.
From the moment that they met
To the day of her death.

Growing up together, I was his protector
Two years older, and his senior
Stood between him and danger

Maybe it was his calling
He was following
When he disappeared into the mountains;
He ascended as Johnny
And some years later
Descended as 'Dread'
'Johnny Dread'
With curly locks, and beard to match
My brother was now a Rasta man.

He was a roamer
A hard worker
A 'ganga' smoker
With lots of brethren and female friends
He was indeed a womanizer
"The girls them sugar"
Who fathered half a dozen children
With quarter dozen mothers.

From East to West
North to South
Throughout the land he was known
Was unique without a doubt
My loving brother
Who now rests with God in peace.

2

RHYTHMS OF LIFE

Life

Life is a journey that we take
Maybe long or maybe short
What's up ahead? Only time will tell.
There may be fortune
There may be fame
May- be - sorrow
Or
May- be - pain
What can we do as we travel along?
Ask God for the courage to carry on.
Be brave!
Be strong!
Be courageous and stand
For life is a journey that's short
Or
L-o-n-g

In This Town

Clock alarming
Man yawning
Day dawning
Cock crowing
Monday morning
Monday morning, Monday morning
Monday morning come
Working time, schooling time
Lord the weekend done!
Same thing day in
Same thing day out
In this dead end town
No recreation, no entertainment
Life remains unchanging

This day like yesterday
Yesterday like the day before
The day before like last week
Last week like the week before
And another Monday morning comes

Rhythm of Life

Out on the street
Everybody that you meet
Dem a hustle, and a bustle,
In the blistering heat.
Trying so hard to make ends meet
Moving here, moving there
To the rhythm and thump
Of their own heart beats

The rhythm is fast
The rhythm is slow
The rhythm is loud
The rhythm is soft
The rhythm is **hard,**
Some missing the beat
But moving still to the rhythm of life
To the rhythm of life they live their lives.

They live their lives to the rhythm of life
The rhythm can be short
The rhythm can be long
But it's all played out
From the beat of the master's hand.

Gone Too Soon

In a flash
Like a snap
In a wink
Like a sigh
It went by.
No traces of the faces
That once laughed and cried.
Now, only memories lingering out of places
That were once occupied and full of life.
Now, they all are faded, deep within the caverns of my mind.
Gone are the days
When life was a smile
And no frowns darken
The brows of friendly faces
drinking in the sunshine.
Where? Oh where did it fly?
When? Oh when did it die?

In a flash
Like a snap…
In a wink…
Like a sigh…
It went by.

Born To Die

From the day of birth
And every day thereafter
Living moves towards a day of dying.

Why then can any man think himself better than another?
We laugh, cry, love and hate
Feel pain, sorrow and even horror.
And when we bleed every blood is the same.

Rich, Poor, black or white and every color in between
All have a date to expire
Captive or free
Prince or pauper
All have hope for a brighter tomorrow
A tomorrow that never comes
Because tomorrow is today
And all there is, is yesterday.

What is done in life, before death finally comes
Is sometimes quickly forgotten
When one enters into eternity

Live, love, laugh, cry and pray
Each and every day
Doing as much good as we should
Because we enter only to exit.

3

UNLOVED

The Meeting

Who is this who has entered my life?
Should I open the door and let her in?
Why is she so interested in been a friend
When there is no friendliness in me?
What is it that draws her in?
Is she a moth and I a flame?
Is this perhaps just a game?
The question really puzzles me.
I want to stay, I want to leave
I know not why.
In the park all by ourselves
My heart took wings and almost flew
I stopped to think.
Is this a gift from God
Or is she from hell?

I Name Man!

I name man,
So I do what I please
I am man, I don't beg on my knees
To please you or no other one
I name man
I do decree.
Woman!..... I name man!
So how you think you can cheat on me with Jim?
And maybe, even with Tom, Dick and Tim.
Do I forgive!
And just pretend?
When you dish me dirt…… it hurts!
Yes I do agree I did it first.
But girls can't do what the guys do, and still be a lady.
No!

I name man
I can't act like a lamb
I name man try to understand
I have no plan to stick around
And be no clown
I gone………… I am man!

The Mirror and I

Tell me truthfully who do you think I am?
(silence)
Mirror, mirror on the wall, did you hear what I asked?
I wait for an answer to satisfy my soul.
Mirror, mirror …..
(reply)
I heard you the first time
I am not deaf, but your question mystifies me!
(speaker)
How so dear mirror, don't you know all things?
Don't you see all things?
(reply)
Oh yes, but what I see you see, and there are more questions than answers you'll find from looking at yourself through me.
And the more you find out the less you'll know.

(speaker)
But all I want to know is who I am!
(reply)
Don't you know? Or, are you pretending not to know.
Look deep in your eyes…. Deep
What reflection do you see?
(speaker)
Nothing!

(reply)
Nothing! You see nothing?
Look deeper
(speaker)
I am looking, but what I see I am not sure is me!
No mirror, you tell me, tell me what you see in me.
(reply)
You sound so confused my dear
But as I've said before, what you see, I see, for
I am only a reflection of yourself
You are the one in the mirror
You are looking at your heart…..
The real real part of you.

(speaker)
My heart, no that's not my heart it cannot be …. Me!
So cold and dark and empty
Alone and full of fear
So hard and void of feelings so…….
Stop, please stop, stop it now
And give to me a true account
For that's not my heart I see!
I am loving, true and kind
And all my friends agree…..
(reply)
You are vain in your imaginations
Oh I wish that you could see,
The love you give is only to your selfish self.
Your heart's not true,
And you have lost identity,
You have lost your way

Pretending to be someone else
Behind painted face

And store bought hair
And sculptured nails
Yourself you cannot see.
Love is just a word you use
And know not the meaning of.
(speaker)
Mirror, mirror on the wall
Help me please to be released
From this cycle of pretence,
And help me find my way
To perfect love and peace.
(reply)
Stop pretending if you dare
And to thy self be true
For true love only comes from God above
The greatest love of all.

Missing

I've missed some things
Not just one thing
But many, many things.

The things I've missed
Are not as painful
like this one important thing.
Which I know I really, really missed!

I've missed the love!
Though I have loved
And have been loved
But never really, really love.
Love has never loved me back,
I gave…
but never did receive.

SUFFERING

The Pain of Emptiness

So deep, so wide, so incomprehensible
It has pledged an oath of allegiance
To be my faithful companion
All my life.

Behind the mask
The black mask of shame and death
Into a black abyss
I feel the pull like a strong magnet

Like a moth to a flame,
I am drowning in a sea of forbidden emotions?
Which are like hungry wolves devouring my tortured soul.
I fight to reach the light
But the light does not befriend me
Will not control me,

Will not envelop me, will not save me from the black
Mask of shame and death

I have lived a lie all my life
Proclaiming to be a child of light
Knowing I am but a child of the dark.
One who speaks truth, yet I know I am false.
The pain is too great; I am tired of the lie.

Where can I run?
Where can I hide?
Who will save me?
Who will change me?
In my pain I have cried out to my father in anguish!
The response is silence…..
Or wait and see
It's not yet time.

Meanwhile I wither and I die
In the prison of my lie,
A desperate, dark and empty life.

I…., have never experienced the joy of free abandonment
Of totally being myself.
Only stolen moments, in the dark, behind closed and battened doors.
Embedded in deep guilt,
I taste what could have been, if I were totally true and free.

I wonder why?
I wonder when?
If I will be redeemed.
Or am I condemned to a place in hell for being created me.

Lord have mercy upon me!
I want to be free to love… without limits
Free to create…. without limits
Free to express my feelings… without limits.
Free to allow the power of the Holy Spirit to walk through me

Without limits.
Alas! I must remain as strong in faith
And boldly stand in Jesus' name, for His Grace
Is sufficient in my earthly pain.

Cry of the Masses

Laud! Laud! laud
Everybody bawling out
Laud! Laud! Laud!
What's it all about?
The times rough!
The times tough!
The times dreadder then dread.
"REPENT!"
For the last days draweth neigh!"
Pastor John Brown shouts.
Blood a go run, revolution now!
The youths dem a bawl, sitting on the wall
"Babylon shall fall!"
The Rasta man chant

The poor can't take no more
Rich man, poor man, beggar man, thief,
Lawyer, doctor, Indian chief
Don't believe, that better will come

Laud! Laud! Laud!
Everybody bawling out
We can't run we can't hide.
Run to the rock!

The rock run gone!
What a thing! What a thing!
What a serious thing!
We get clap.
Imagine that, we get clap!
Like a rat in a trap, we get clap,
A-relly-bap, a-relly –bap
We get clap
Clap, clap, clap
Laud! laud! laud!
Everybody bawling out,

"Let not your heart be troubled"
Pastor John Brown whisper in a whimper

Trapped

Like a caged bird
Or a captured stallion rearing to go,
I cannot break free
From these bonds in which the net of life
Has captured me.
I want to run like a deer
And fly like an eagle
and be free of this place that has captured me.
I am caught in this place with no roads leading out
Trapped in past memories, with no future hope.
I am a living dead!

I Cry To Myself

I cry to myself
On the outside looking in
On the inside of me.
I am trapped in a place called the graveyard of dreams
And silently suffers by myself.

I cry to myself for myself, and no one sees the invisible tears
Or hear the silent screams
Or see me reaching out for help in a cold indifferent world
Where hope is lost and care is dead.

I cry to myself for myself
For I am lost there's no way out,
For I have travelled too far I fear
Down a dark and dreadful road
I think I missed a turn
I cry to myself for myself
From a desperate lonely heart that dies with every beat.

Reading Rapp

Reading is a very good thing
Reading is a natural thing
Reading takes you near and far
You don't even have to ride in a car.

Read for entertainment
Read for satisfaction
And get into the action!

Bad things happen when you cannot read….
Read and write and multiply.
Learn how to read, and learn how to write
It will take you far in life.

Teacher! Teacher!
I have a story to tell!
A story to tell?
Yes a story to tell,

It's about a boy name Fred!
Once upon a- time, not a very long- time
Fred banged his head and he was dead,
Just because he couldn't read or spell.
Fred played the fool by saying he's cool
And just would never, never stay in school.

The sign at the pool read
'No diving at this shallow end'
Not knowing what it had said.
In dove Fred and damaged his head.
And that was the end of my good friend Fred!
Oh what a fool
He died in the pool
Thinking he was oh so cool!

The Old Blind Beggar

When was it that I became aware of him?
The old blind beggar sitting on the side of the road?

Was it morning, noon, or evening time?
As I daily pass that way on my ups and downs.

It was the sound of despair
Coming from a thirsty throat
Begging for a drink
That made me stop, to look and think.

I turned my head
And there I saw him like the dead
hand outstretched from where he sat
A beggar man sitting on a dirty mat.
His eyes not seeing
But he was hearing
Everyone that passed him by
Not caring.

I thought, and thought
And then across the road I walked
To buy the coldest bottled water I think
For him to drink.

He drank and sighed so deep
My heart did sink
To think of all his pain and suffering.
In his outstretched hand I did release
A fist full of coins.
How mush is this? He smiled and asked
Not much I said, but you'll be fed.
He whispered low, to me he said
May God be praised and you be blessed.

Sing! Sing! Africa!

Africa!
Mother Africa.
Our voices are raised
To sing a praise to God for you
For keeping us through the passage of our darkened history.
Africa the land of our fore-fathers and the fathers before them.
Whose journey was long and hard, but God our help in ages past,
Our hope for years to come,
Has been our shelter in the dreadful, hateful, wicked times of slavery.

Africa! Oh Africa!
The blood that our fore-fathers shed
The tears that our fore-mothers cried
Have watered fields of banana, cotton and sugar cane.

Lost beneath the ocean depths
The souls the passage did destroy
Their pain I feel within my breast

The years have not erased the awful crime of slavery.
With steadfast hope, and fervent prayers
Our God did set us free
Like the Israelites who once were bound in Egypt's iron grip.

Rejoice! Rejoice! oh Africa for God has kept your children strong
Despite our pain and suffering
Though from the bitter, bitter cup we drank.
As he himself had walked the path
Oh sweet the Rose of Sharon
On whom we cast our cares
That kept our spirits free as air
Though feet and hands were bound with chains.
And when the masters' whip did crack
And tore the skin from off our backs
My Jesus did break through the pain
For this he clearly understood
To become our balm in Gilead

Africa! Mother Africa.
The Negro race has risen
Like a Phoenix from the ash
With head and shoulders high
To stand up tall, to give God praise
And let all nations know
That God has kept us all the way
That's why we're here today

Flesh And Spirit

Flesh and spirit live together
Yet they never can unite,
Always fighting with each other
No matter if it's day or night.

Which is stronger?
I'm left to wonder
Either one will have its way
No matter what you want to say.

One controls the outer realm
The other controls the inner soul
So an epic battle rages on
From the tragic fall of man
And will continue all through life.

Flesh is built upon emotions
Spirit upon faith and hope
The two sides of a coin.
One is fighting to destroy
The other fighting to purify
The fragile heart of man.

The choice that all man has to make
Is which will mold their destiny,
For one of them must lead to utter darkness
The other to eternal light.

5

ESCAPE

Frozen People, Frozen Town

I long for the day
I long for the day
When my brothers and my sisters
Will wake to see the light
Frozen people, frozen town
This town lord! It gets me down
Frozen people, frozen town
Nobody seems to know where they are bound.
This town is asleep
But who holds the keys
To set these prisoners free?
Don't despair a voice above me say
Don't give up the fight
Behind the cloud there's a silver line
Life is just no easy game
Win or loose
God remains the same.

A Stranger In The Land

Everything has changed
There are no familiar faces
Hardly any familiar places
I am a stranger in the land of my birth.

Many years have passed since I came back to be
A strange on an alien shore.
Peopled by beings in love with material stuff
Who worship at the shrine of money and lust.

All is not lost, I desire to hear
From those whom still hold the culture dear
For, it's only by understanding the past
That the future may be bright at last.

I am a stranger in the land
Separated from the past
I hope all, is not lost.

Chasing After You!

Boom Boom Shack!
Boom Boom Shack
Boom Shaka Lack!

Boom Boom Shack
Boom Boom Shack
Boom Shaka Lack
Give me you Lord!.....
Boom Boom Shack
Give me you! Shack… Boom Shaka Lack
I' m Chasing after you.

Give me you lord!....... Boom Boom Shack
Give me you Shack, Boom Shaka lack
I'm chasing after you…… I'm chasing after you

Only you can fill my soul
Only you can make me whole.
You are the Lord, the one true God
You are the one, almighty one
This is a truth I can't deny
I'm chasing after you

When will it end?
There is no end my friend
Not even when you're dead
I seek and I will find
I knock and don't look back
I have to find I have to find
No leaving me behind.

The paths of righteousness is mine
No longer blind for now I see.
I'm chasing after you!

I'm chasing after you!
My hope is built on nothing less
I'm chasing after you!
Give me you, Shack, Boom Boom Shack
Give me you, Shack, Boom Shaka lack!
Nothing else will do!
I'm chasing after you!
My lord and savor Jesus Christ
I'm chasing after you!
BOOM!

Free

I am free
Free at last
From appointments
Schedules and tasks.
Free from the imprisoned limits of time
Of the twenty four seven games of mine.
Free to be still as yielded clay
In the master potter's hand I stay
Free I say,
I am free at last!

www.ingramcontent.com/pod-product-compliance
Lightning Source LLC
LaVergne TN
LVHW092059060526
838201LV00047B/1474